DISCOVER ANCIENT CIVILIZATIONS

Ancient Rome

by M.J. York

CAPSTONE VALUE LIBRARY
a capstone imprint

Published by Capstone® Value Library, an imprint of Capstone
1710 Roe Crest Drive, North Mankato, Minnesota 56003
capstonepub.com

Library of Congress Cataloging-in-Publication Data is available on the Library of Congress website
ISBN: 9798875306679 (hardcover)
ISBN: 9798875306686 (ebook PDF)

Summary: An exploration of the history and legacy of ancient Rome.

Editorial Credits
Editor: Kellie M. Hultgren; Designer: Jennifer Walker; Production Specialist: Tori Abraham

Image Credits
Dreamstime: Davidglinn, 23, Sborisov, cover; Getty Images: javarman3, 13; Shutterstock: AlexAnton, 5, Emily Marie Wilson, 21, Ivan Moreno sl, 17, V_E, 9, zcebeci, 7

Printed and bound in the USA. 006585

Table of Contents

CHAPTER 1

Ancient Rome

Ancient Rome began on the banks of the Tiber River in what is Italy today. People had long hunted and farmed in the area. By the 800s BCE, they had built villages on seven hills there. Over centuries, the civilization grew. Its **legions** conquered near and far to expand the empire. **Engineers** built roads and buildings that still stand today.

At its height, the city of Rome felt like the center of the world. People came there from across the empire. They wrote poetry and plays. They watched **gladiator** fights. They spoke Latin and worshipped many gods and goddesses.

The Colosseum in Rome is one of the most famous ancient Roman buildings.

CHAPTER 2

From Farms to an Empire

Rome began as farming villages on a riverbank. By the 200s BCE, Romans had conquered the whole Italian **peninsula**. Then the empire spread. At its largest, the Roman Empire stretched from Britain to the Middle East. It circled the Mediterranean Sea, controlling Europe as well as northern Africa. Trade routes stretched deep into Africa and across Asia and Europe. Grain came from Egypt and olive oil from Spain.

Roads connected the empire's cities. The land was divided into provinces. A governor from Rome led each province. Even though they had been conquered, people in the provinces could keep their native languages and gods. Eventually they could become **citizens** of Rome.

Part of a Roman road remains near the ancient city of Tarsus in what is now the country of Türkiye.

CHAPTER 3

The Roman Republic

In the early years, kings likely ruled the Roman people. By the 500s BCE, the people had formed a new type of government. They called it a republic. *Republic* comes from two Latin words, *res* and *publica*. It means "matters of the public." Instead of a king, a group of men ran the government. Two consuls led the group for a one-year term. They were elected.

Senators met in the senate to make laws and decisions. They were all wealthy men. They often governed to make themselves wealthier. Poorer men revolted. They formed a second group called the assembly. They demanded that the government help the lower classes.

The Roman government was run from the Forum, a group of important buildings around a public square in Rome.

However, the Roman **economy** rested on slavery. Enslaved people worked all types of jobs, from mining and farming to tutoring wealthy children. Military captives were enslaved. Traders bought and sold enslaved people across the empire.

Age of Empire

Famous general Julius Caesar won many battles and gathered military strength for himself. The senate worried he would make himself a king. In 44 BCE, a group of senators **assassinated** Caesar. However, Caesar's adopted son Octavian took control. In 27 BCE, Octavian renamed himself Augustus Caesar. Rome now had an emperor.

Legions fought battles on the empire's edges. But within the empire it was more peaceful. Many people **prospered**.

Emperors ruled the Roman empire for several centuries more. Eventually the empire split into eastern and western halves. The western empire ended in 476 CE, when the last emperor lost his throne. The eastern empire continued for another thousand years.

CHAPTER 4

Home and Family

Family was important in Roman society. The father was the head of the family. He had legal control over the rest of the family. Women could not hold government power. But they ran their households, and they could hold jobs.

In Rome, poorer people lived in apartments. These buildings could be five stories tall or more. The ground floor was often a shop or workshop. A middle class house had several rooms and a central courtyard with no roof. Wealthy Romans lived in **villas** and palaces.

The courtyard of a merchant's home in Pompeii has beautiful paintings and a fountain with mosaic decorations.

Roman Life

Romans ate a lot of wheat and bread. Olive oil, wine, lentils, seafood, and vegetables were important. Meat was more expensive. The city had to **import** food to feed its many people.

Roman men wore togas for formal occasions. The toga is like a large wool sheet. It is worn draped over one shoulder. Men wore knee-length belted shirts, called tunics, for working. Women wore tunics and skirts. An overdress called a stola showed a woman was married.

Most Roman parents taught their children a trade or skill. Many people never learned to read. Wealthy families often owned an enslaved tutor. Some middle-class families paid for school. Students learned reading, math, and literature. Few girls went to school.

CHAPTER 5

Art and Science

Roman art survives today in statues, stone carvings, **mosaics**, and wall paintings. Roman artists often borrowed from older Greek styles.

Many writings survive from Roman times. Plays, poems, and other works teach us about daily life, religion, and politics. Some are even funny!

Romans built with brick, stone, and concrete. They built aqueducts with arches to bring water into the cities. Beautiful temples with large domes and tall columns awed worshippers.

Romans relaxed in public bathhouses. They watched gladiators fight animals and warriors in amphitheaters. Chariots raced around a giant track called a circus. Romans did not have weekends, but they had many holidays and festivals.

Military Technology

The empire grew because of the Roman army. Men from across the empire joined the army. The legions were organized into smaller units. The troops were highly trained.

Each soldier had armor and weapons to match his troop's fighting style. Some fought with swords and spears. Some rode horses or shot arrows. Others broke down enemy walls with catapults.

A marble carving from the first century BCE shows members of important Roman families wearing their best clothes.

Army engineers built paved roads as straight as possible. Arched bridges crossed rivers. This let the armies travel swiftly. In peacetime the roads united the empire. Large walls protected forts and cities.

CHAPTER 6

Gods and Goddesses

Romans worshipped many gods and goddesses. Roman religion borrowed much from Greek mythology. Jupiter, king of the gods, was like the Greek god Zeus. Minerva, goddess of wisdom, was like the Greek Athena. Mars, god of war, was important to the military-minded Romans.

Performing ceremonies helped Romans gain favor from the gods. Each festival had specific **rituals**. People ate special foods or paraded statues through the streets.

Roman families kept small statues to honor personal gods. These spirits were sometimes ancestors. Romans believed that these statues gave good luck and protected the family's home.

The people of the empire could worship almost any god they chose. But everyone was supposed to make offerings to the emperor too. Religious groups that refused, including Christians, were punished. But by the 300s CE, the empire became officially Christian.

Roman citizens in Dougga, in what is now Tunisia in northern Africa, worshipped in this temple to Jupiter, Juno, and Minerva.

CHAPTER 7

The Legacy of Rome

Roman language, literature, and ways of thinking shaped European culture. During the Renaissance in the 1500s CE, artists looked back to Rome's art, architecture, and science.

Tourists still walk roads and tour buildings built throughout the empire. At the Colosseum in Rome, visitors imagine ancient gladiator fights. They climb Hadrian's Wall in northern England at the edge of the empire. Researchers study Pompeii and Herculaneum, where a volcano eruption happened in 79 CE. It preserved much information about daily life. These pieces of ancient Rome have a powerful influence today.

The streets of Herculaneum, with public fountains, shops, and homes, give modern tourists a glimpse of Roman daily life.

Glossary

assassinated (uh-SASS-uh-nay-tuhd)—killed, often for power or political reasons

citizens (SI-tuh-zuhnz)—members of a state or people who can participate in a government

economy (i-KAH-nuh-mee)—structure of money, trade, taxes, and goods in a country or region

engineers (en-juh-NEERZ)—designers or builders of structures or devices

gladiator (GLAD-ee-ay-tur)—Ancient Roman enslaved person trained to fight in public battles for entertainment

import (IM-port)—goods brought or sold into a country or region

legions (LEE-juhnz)—units of foot soldiers in the Roman army

mosaics (moh-ZAY-ikz)—designs or patterns made by applying small pieces of tile, glass, or stone to a surface

peninsula (puh-NIN-suh-luh)—portion of land mostly surrounded by water

prospered (PROSS-prd)—were strong and flourishing

rituals (RICH-oo-uhlz)—established forms, actions, or words of a ceremony

villas (VIL-uhz)—large and luxurious homes, often in the country

Index